In the Shado

In the Shadow of Mount Sinai

A Footnote on the Origins and Changing Forms of Total Membership

Peter Sloterdijk

Translated by Wieland Hoban

polity

First published in German as *Im Schatten des Sinai: Fußnote über Ursprünge und Wandlungen totaler Mitgliedschaft*, © Suhrkamp Verlag, Berlin, 2013
This English edition © Polity Press, 2016

Polity Press
65 Bridge Street
Cambridge CB2 1UR, UK

Polity Press
350 Main Street
Malden, MA 02148, USA

All rights reserved. Except for the quotation of short passages for the purpose of criticism and review, no part of this publication may be reproduced, stored in a retrieval system, or transmitted, in any form or by any means, electronic, mechanical, photocopying, recording or otherwise, without the prior permission of the publisher.

ISBN-13: 978-0-7456-9923-3
ISBN-13: 978-0-7456-9924-0 (pb)

A catalogue record for this book is available from the British Library.

Library of Congress Cataloging-in-Publication Data

Sloterdijk, Peter, 1947-
[Im Schatten des Sinai. English]
In the shadow of Mount Sinai / Peter Sloterdijk. -- English edition.
pages cm
Includes bibliographical references and index.
ISBN 978-0-7456-9923-3 (hardback : alk. paper) -- ISBN 978-0-7456-9924-0 (pbk. : alk. paper) 1. Religious fundamentalism--Political aspects.
2. Religious fundamentalism--Social aspects. 3. Anger--Religious aspects.
4. Philosophical anthropology. I. Title.
BL238.S56813 2015
201'.4--dc23
2015007555

Typeset in 12.5 on 15 pt Adobe Garamond by
Servis Filmsetting Ltd, Stockport, Cheshire
Printed and bound in the UK by CPI Group (UK) Ltd, Croydon

The publisher has used its best endeavours to ensure that the URLs for external websites referred to in this book are correct and active at the time of going to press. However, the publisher has no responsibility for the websites and can make no guarantee that a site will remain live or that the content is or will remain appropriate.

Every effort has been made to trace all copyright holders, but if any have been inadvertently overlooked the publisher will be pleased to include any necessary credits in any subsequent reprint or edition.

For further information on Polity, visit our website:
politybooks.com

Contents

I

Narrowing the Battle Zone

Anyone planning to say something about a controversial matter such as the violent implications of what we call 'monotheism', both those proven and those merely asserted, would be well advised to follow a few rules of caution. Theology is demonic terrain. What Thomas Mann noted about music in his big Washington speech of 1945 about 'Germany and the Germans' applies no less to speaking about divine matters and about this-worldly and other-worldly things. The observation made in the same speech that music is 'the most remote from reality of all the arts and, at the same time, the most passionate' can be transferred without any noteworthy changes to the nature of many theological lessons. They often deal with the most distant and evasive factors, such as God, omnipotence, salvation and damnation, with a vehemence that only the most intimate motifs of passion can ignite. What music and theology have in common is that, when things get serious, they can both be closer to the affected person than the person themselves – as expressed by Saint Augustine in his confessional phrase *interior intimo meo* ('more inward than the most inward place in my heart').[1]

With this warning in mind, I would like in the following to jot down some reflections that can be read as footnotes to two of my religio-theoretical publications from recent years: *God's Zeal*[2] and *You Must Change Your Life*.[3] Nonetheless, the deliberations below should also be comprehensible without reference to these books. Some of the theologians' reactions to *God's Zeal* reminded me that one evidently cannot raise certain topics without bringing them to life through such a

[1] Augustine, *Confessions*, trans. Frank J. Sheed, ed. Michael P. Foley (Indianapolis: Hackett, 2006), p. 44.

[2] Peter Sloterdijk, *God's Zeal: The Battle of the Three Monotheisms*, trans. Wieland Hoban (Cambridge: Polity, 2009).

[3] Peter Sloterdijk, *You Must Change Your Life: On Anthropotechnics*, trans. Wieland Hoban (Cambridge: Polity, 2013).

discussion. It seems that, by speaking of religious zeal systems in the monotheisms, I had aroused an inclination towards zealous rebuttal, or even the warding-off of demons, among certain readers, namely those from Christian theological circles. These 'rebuttals' generally proceeded from the allegation that I had indiscriminately ascribed to the monotheistic 'scriptural religions', namely Judaism, Christianity and Islam, an 'intrinsic' (thus the established debating term) or, differently put, an irremovable violent component, thus confusing the timelessly benign essence of these religions with their sometimes unappealing historical manifestations. The most determined opponents of this thesis they themselves had posited countered it with the claim that the aforementioned religions, Christianity in particular, wanted to be understood both in their nature and in their self-image as liberating and peacemaking movements. They had, however, been temporarily distracted from their authentic mission by heretical distortions and political instrumentalizations in the course of their respective histories.

In the light of the discussion's development, which was characterized largely by projections,

misreading and apologetic interests – and aug-
mented by the numerous, usually very interesting
reactions to Jan Assmann's theses on the 'Mosaic
distinction' published slightly earlier – I began
to doubt that it would be productive to continue
the debate as an argument over the correct use
of the term 'monotheism'. Above all, the oppo-
sition cited *ad nauseam* between a purportedly
violence-inclined monotheism and a purportedly
violence-averse polytheism constituted a carica-
ture that is best met with silence. In the following
remarks, then, I will avoid the term 'monotheism'
as far as possible[4] and focus instead on discuss-
ing the phenomenon of zealous and potentially
violently manifested motivation with reference
to certain religious norms without addressing
once again the logical construction of the one-

[4] Concerning the distinction between relevant concepts such
as henotheism, summotheism, monolatry, the 'Yahweh alone
movement', poly-Yahwism, inclusive, exclusive, prophetic, practical and philosophical monotheism, and so on, see Michaela
Bauks, 'Monotheismus (AT)', in *Wissenschaftliches Bibellexikon
(WiBiLex)*, ed. Deutsche Bibelgesellschaft, available at www.
bibelwissenschaft.de/wibilex/das-bibellexikon (accessed 12
January 2015); Bernhard Lang, 'Monotheismus', in *Handbuch
religionswissenschaftlicher Grundbegriffe*, vol. 4: *Kultbild – Rolle*,
ed. Hubert Cancik, Burkhard Gladigow and Karl-Heinz Kohl
(Stuttgart: Kohlhammer, 1998), pp. 148–65.

God faith.[5] I will also put aside my reservations about the term 'religion', which were explained in *You Must Change Your Life* (I consider it a pseudo-term or, more precisely, a false abstraction with a high potential to mislead) and use the term conventionally and without irony here and on the following pages, as I do not wish to complicate the already sufficiently controversial topic by opening a second front. I therefore cannot engage with the accusation that the latter work of mine is 'the most fundamental attack on religion since Feuerbach'[6] – which would be an ambiguous complement in the best case, but in reality constitutes a polemical warning call to the rest of the theological world. For the moment, I shall make do with noting that the practice-theoretical reflections in *You Must Change Your Life* are precisely not an attack on religion but rather a sympathetic attempt to explore the facts of the religious field through a second description

[5] More on this and the thought figure *secundum non datur* in *God's Zeal*, ch. 5, 'The Matrix', pp. 82–104. There I develop the thesis that the phenomenon of zeal not only has psychologically relevant motives but is also based on a logical grammar.

[6] Klaus Müller, 'Generalangriff im Tarnanzug: Peter Sloterdijk über Religion', in *Communicatio Socialis* 42/4 (2009), pp. 345f.

that stays close to its object – in the language of a general practice theory, albeit combined with the aim of contributing to a clarification of the misunderstanding of religions consolidated on all sides.[7]

In the present essay, I operate on the assumption that it is not the single or plural nature of conceptions of God among collectives or individuals that plays the decisive part in releasing acts of violence. Rather, what determines a disposition towards the use of violence is the form and intensity of the absorption of faith practisers by the system of norms to which they subordinate their existence. If the term 'monotheism' still crops up

[7] Practice should be understood as autoplastic action, meaning a kind that acts back on the actor. Without consideration of practice aspects, acculturation processes in general are as incomprehensible as religio-ritual phenomena in particular. The general theory of practice can be directly related to the humanities and social sciences, as it makes no unnecessary concessions to naturalism. It consistently rests on culture-theoretical premises, though it emphasizes the aspect that 'culture' would remain an empty term without examining the dimension of incorporation procedures. The cliff of reductionism is avoided by introducing the theory of practice (as a hermeneutics of repetition) into a shared understanding of cultural, especially theopoetic procedures. If practice analysis initially unsettles theologians, this is probably because it deals less with questions of truth than with states of being-in-shape.

occasionally in the following reflections, then, it refers not so much to a group of theological or metaphysical conceptions. To the extent that it cannot be entirely avoided, I use it for the time being simply as a historically successful complex of heightened psycho-religious motivation.

2

On the Genesis of Peoples in General

There is surely still a consensus in the science of religion that early religious cult systems – whatever else they might be – can be viewed in their primary manner of effect as ethnoplastic systems of rules. By imposing shared narratives, rituals and norms on a collective, they mould the practising collectives into carriers – into the subject-object, philosophically speaking – of those same conceptions and procedures. Thus the phenomenon of religion (in the era before its individualistic differentiation in modernity, at least) seems initially to be tied entirely to the time-honoured functions of group synthesis. The biological reproduction of a 'culture' or ethnic collective is necessarily accompanied by the passing on of the group-specific system of symbols and rituals.

The fact that these simple observations lead to non-trivial consequences can be clarified by the following reflections. It is no coincidence that ethnologists, anthropologists and theologians have been claiming for some time that no indications have been found anywhere in the world pointing to the existence of completely 'irreligious peoples' – and how could they, when the phenomenon of peoples as such is engendered only by the collective-integrative effects of shared rites and histories, conventionally known as 'religions'. The assumption of a people existing completely without religion would amount to the paradoxical assertion that there can be stabilized collectives which dispense with all connecting media and do not become acquainted with any symbolic bond, shared history or firm normative commitments. This would mean virtually postulating a people devoid of content – and thus more a random crowd than a physically and spiritually self-reproducing unit.

For the same reason, a people in any meaningful sense of the word thus cannot exist without its language – provided one understands language not merely as a vehicle for everyday communication but also, and most importantly, as a medium for imprinting the most culturally important subjects on the consciousness of its speakers. From this perspective, language is primarily the organ of relevance. Humans can only claim to speak a language properly once they can say in it what is vital for life. Naturally, this highest level of relevance always includes local ideas about the collective's conditions of survival and salvation. Thoughts about this are not exchanged in passing under the palaver tree or the well but are usually etched in the memories of a collective's members in moments of terrible seriousness, often in emotional stress situations resulting from bloody sacrificial acts. In the history of cultures so far, the establishment of the highest-ranking motifs of relevance has often been connected to procedures enforcing a pedagogy of pain and suffering.[8]

There is no need to expand on why, among

[8] Only recently did it become possible to counter the immemorial pain-based training techniques in socialization with psychological arguments. Thus Bruno Bettelheim fundamentally denied the positive effects of painful inculcations during initiations. And Michael Balint goes so far as to say: 'It is suffering that makes one wicked' (Michael Balint, *Primary Love and Psycho-Analytic Technique* [London: Routledge, 2001], p. 49).

the notions significant for salvation and survival that are passed on through language and rites within the internal space of an ethnicity, it is the instructions for preserving differences of status that almost always play an outstanding part. In early folk religions, making leadership positions imposing was one of the sources of the sacred. To ensure hierarchical control over the collective, most early peoples cloaked the chief and leader roles, and later the royal ranks, with an aura of sacred import and bestowed upon them the power to determine the life or death of their own people as well as strangers. One can generally observe that the preferred activity of early religions was concerning themselves with the sacralization of leadership.[9] In addition, they

[9] The psychology of religion attributes the inclination towards the sacralization of leadership roles to paleopsychic hereditary dispositions: 'As all primates develop hierarchies and the higher-ranking group members have defensive functions, one can presume an instinctive willingness to seek shelter among the higher ranks. When this need is not met, because the respected individuals themselves feel a need for protection, imaginarily high-ranking figures can close the perceived gap in the security system by way of fiction. If the symbolic regulating mechanisms constitute themselves via the cult of such projectively produced leader figures, this is connected to the fact that living figures of authority inherited their institution's rules from earlier authorities, meaning that the respective role of authority

focused on the symbolic aggrandizement and cultic securing of protective spaces, burial sites and important foodstuffs.

Related thoughts manifest themselves in Johann Gottfried Herder's suggestive remark that, 'among the most uncultivated people, the language of religion is ever the most ancient and obscure.'[10] The increasing opacity of older religious languages is substantially due to the fact that, in the course of the civilization process, some gestures and turns of phrase are forgotten that were previously required in order to commit the collective to its own inner cohesion and ideas of sacred relevance. Such figures are later carried along erratically by the current of sacred traditions as petrified relics of an obsolete self-constraint. As one can observe from the seventeenth century on in Europe, modernizing cultures subject themselves to an accelerated change in the forms of

is a cross-generational archetype that no human individual can embody in the long term. Hence a people's gods are identical to the prototypical roles that have to be filled anew in each generation. (Gerhard Baudy, 'Kultobjekt', in *Handbuch religionswissenschaftlicher Grundbegriffe*, vol. 4: *Kultbild – Rolle*, pp. 28f.)

[10] Johann Gottfried Herder, *Reflections on the Philosophy of the History of Mankind*, trans. T. O. Churchill (Chicago and London: University of Chicago Press, 1968), p. 350.

self-constraint (especially following the replacement of the sacred victim constraint by secular institutes such as the constraints of schooling and taxation), with the inevitable result that participants in modern social games no longer perceive earlier methods of alignment merely as venerable relics, but increasingly as dark embarrassments.

With these stenographic intimations of early ethnogenesis through intra-ethnic narratives, rites and salvific notions, I am attempting to explain plausibly why, and using what concepts, the recent science of 'ethnology' was able to move beyond Platonizing views of ethnic archetypes and beyond Romantic ideas relating to the 'spirits of peoples'. However generously Herder's ethnological ecumenism was conceived, with all ethnicities of the world, their confused literature about gods and their sonorous folk song inventions considered colours in the prism of an absolute creativity, it remained problematic in its essentialist view of peoples as spiritual-cultural substances that emanated – no one knows how – from the transcendent productivity of the world's creator.

Once peoples have entered existence, however primitive they might be, they can, in the further course of their development, follow the routines of generational shift that – in the triad of theme, variation and reflection – produce cultural convention. Thus Herder, following his own premises, not only very rightly raised the question 'Whence is the religion of these people derived? Can these poor creatures have invented their religious worship as a sort of natural theology?'[11] He could also answer it using on-board – that is to say, immanent and culture-historical means: 'absorbed in labour, they invent nothing, but in all things follow the traditions of their forefathers.'[12] 'Here therefore *tradition has been the propagator of their religion and sacred rites, as of their language and slight degree of civilization.*'[13] For Herder too, then, the enigma of religion lies not so much in its horizontal transmission through the stream of generations; rather, it conceals itself in the unobservable, almost vertical beginning of ethnogeneses. Herder makes no secret of his view that all peoples, even the materially poorest and the culturally least developed, must be understood

[11] Ibid., p. 349.
[12] Ibid.
[13] Ibid., p. 350.

as genuine ideas of God. In their own respective
ways, they all hear the grand melody. It is therefore no surprise that these actually existing ideas
have reflected upon themselves since time immemorial. Where there is a people, there is always
also the crystallization nucleus of a religion; and
where there is religion, the embodiment of the
creating divine is implied by a special language-
based ethnic manifestation. Because, from the
perspective of this over-eager cultural theology,
peoples *per se* carry divine sparks inside themselves, it is in their nature to speak as theopoetic
collectives. In doing so, they manifest themselves
at wildly varying degrees of explicitness as local
carriers of a potentially generalizable idea of God.

It should be clear that, with this generous interpretation of global ethnic diversity, the Weimar
consistorial councillor Herder was following
on, consciously or unconsciously, from the theology of Pentecost.[14] At the same time – as a
child of the Enlightenment and a partisan of the
French Revolution – he disconnects the remarkable incident on the fiftieth day after the Jesuan
Passover from the original scene in Jerusalem and

[14] Acts 2: 1–41.

stretches it geographically and historically into a worldwide, ever-repeating event. From an idea-historical perspective, Herder's theory of peoples is typical of his time: a synthesis of the Christian doctrine of spirit and the extra-Christian theory of genius. As individual brilliance manifests itself in works of art, the brilliance of peoples manifests itself in religions.

It was in the nature of the topic that Herder's enthusiastic interpretation of ethnic pluralism could not be the last word on the matter. Anyone who speaks of a 'people' *eo ipso* speaks of 'peoples', and whoever speaks of 'peoples' cannot avoid asking what are the principles of its continued existence, which also means the mechanisms of its separation, its multiplication, its decline, its interdependence and its mixture. This and nothing else is the aim of the discipline that in the late nineteenth century was given the name 'ethnology' and since the early twentieth has been known as 'cultural anthropology'. Its task is to study ethnogenetic processes in the light of secular premises. It goes without saying that this entails the abandonment of popular concepts based on essentialist or even metaphysical foundations. This brings the mythopoetic and theopoetic talents of peoples to light all the more clearly.[15]

The matter itself and the mental disquiet accompanying it go back to antiquity. Humanity did not need to await the appearance of cultural anthropologists in order to become aware of the facts of religious and ethnic pluralism. Just how old the beleaguered awareness of the existence of a multiethnic problem really is is demonstrated by, among other things, the myth of the Tower of Babel. The authors of this equally brief and momentous tale[16] (which, according to current research, was inserted into the Book of Genesis [*Bereshit*] in the Pentateuch in post-exilic times, meaning at the

[15] Upon studying ethnogeneses using non-essentialist premises, previously neglected phenomena such as mixture, hybridization, assimilation, transformation, pseudology, disintegration and new formation become especially apparent. In the units termed 'peoples', the metamorphoses are often more impressive than the continuities, the plasticity more impressive than the constancy, and the absorption capacity more impressive than the immunity to foreign elements. Ethnopurists will be especially surprised by the new formation of peoples that emerge from mixtures between diverse ethnic remainders; see Wilhelm Emil Mühlmann, 'Colluvies gentium: Volksentstehung aus Asylen', in *Homo creator: Abhandlungen zur Soziologie, Anthropologie und Ethnologie* (Wiesbaden: Harrassowitz, 1962), pp. 303–10.

[16] Genesis II: 1–9.

dawn of the sixth century) made it easier for themselves to access the problematic issue by placing the bold assumption of a monolingual humanity at the start. The editors of the tower myth, priests returning to Palestine from Babylon who saw no reason to hide their anti-imperial affect, simply equated monolinguality with unanimity and unanimity with despicable arrogance. From the clerical perspective, arrogance leads directly to self-deification. In the architectural dialect, this results in the decision to erect a tower reaching up to heaven. It is no surprise that this displeases a Jewish God from Sinai, here already dated back to prehistory. In his wrath he shatters the languages of the builders, thus causing them to scatter in all directions – until finally, for better or worse, seventy-two peoples with as many languages and cults settle on the earth, sufficiently far apart and deeply inwardly estranged from one another.[17] The nuisance of ethnic plurality is attributed to the preventative punishment of the arrogance that manifests itself in buildings of urbane magnificence.

[17] See Arno Borst, *Der Turmbau von Babel: Geschichte der Meinungen über Ursprung und Vielfalt der Sprachen und Völker* [1957–63], 4 vols (Munich: dtv, 1995).

From the era of early empire-formations, if not even earlier, the awareness of the simultaneous existence of many peoples already articulated succinctly in ancient times took on a high degree of religio-political virulence. Indeed, the thinkers among early peoples did not fail to recognize the connection between the existence of ethnic groupings and securing them through religious cults. Nonetheless, the ancient world did not yet have ecumenical forums to discuss the rivalry and coexistence of the gods, let alone any ethnological overviews of converging and diverging variants of cults devoted to higher beings – to say nothing of the touristic and academic neutralization of differences between peoples and myths, which did not spread outwards from Europe until the eighteenth century.

In the era of increasingly nervous encounters between peoples in the second and first millennia BC, there were various attempts to come to terms with the irreducible pluralism of ethnicities and their religioid control systems. At a general level, one can divide these attempts into two opposing blocks of neighbourhood policies. On the one side are syncretistic tendencies whose goal is a liberating amalgamation of foreign worlds of peoples and gods. Unifying tendencies of this kind are typical of political theologies such as those attempted in the integration of several ethnicities into an empire and a corresponding higher-level sacred imperial order. In the process, priests of a local cult are retrained as diplomats who can recognize their own gods under the foreign names they bear in other popular cults. The great innovation of this school of thought lies in the discovery that, with interculturally sustainable gods, the inner and the outer converge: what one had taken for a foreign god is revealed, upon closer inspection, as a different guise of one's own deity. Peoples and cults approach one another as soon as they understand that they have devoted themselves to the same numinous entity under different names. The ecumenically compatible thought model of the one in the many spread among the educated, and the number one became the keyword in educated synthesis. Thus imperial theology, whether Egyptian, Mesopotamian, Hellenistic or Roman, emerged as the field in which the traditional distinction between domestic and foreign policy faded. That translations between the cults were usually supported by the monarchs and priesthoods of trans-ethnic state constructions is a result of their unmistaken interest in synthetic concepts and ecumenical solutions.

A completely different interpretation of the polyethnic and multicultic situation can be observed in the second block. Here the leading actors respond to the perception of polyethnic existence with a resolute hardening and aggrandizement of their own cult traditions. This tendency to withdraw to what is their own culminates in the refusal to let oneself be compared and to participate in translations. Hence the alternative way out of the inevitable ethnic and cultic comparison invites an escape to singularity. Anyone recommending this strategy for self-preservation amid intercultic competition to a people must also offer the prospect of a great contest: because our god is like no other, our people too will be like no other. Whoever commits to the untranslatable god, the most exclusive of divinities, will be rewarded with endless procreative successes and offspring with long memories. Whoever does not join the confessional community may go under amid the multiplicity, leaving neither traces nor memories behind – biblically put, their name will be struck from the Book of Life.

It is surely unnecessary to emphasize that the

second of these paths was the option of Israel when it decided against the danger of confusion allegedly posed first by living among the Egyptians, then by the encounters with Near Eastern peoples who followed different cults.[18] The often discussed ban on images, which rules out cultic depictions of the Jewish god, initially testifies not so much to the theological depth of a new concept of God as to the ingenious realization that the most reliable way to stay free of the confusing cult competition is the consistent non-depiction of one's own god. In his non-manifestation, the leaders of the Jewish people found a remarkable and unique selling point that ensured incomparability through invisibility. Whether this concept was influenced by Egyptian models or not was of no consequence for its success. The resulting theological problem, namely the incompatibility of the image ban with the epiphanic imperative – that is, the obligation of any god with worldly competence to appear – was taken on board by the creators of the Jewish religion.

[18] Klaus Koch, *Der Gott Israels und die Götter des Orients: Religionsgeschichtliche Studien II* (Göttingen: Vandenhoeck & Ruprecht, 2007), esp. pp. 9–41.

At this point in our reflections, it requires no great effort to explain why the term 'monotheism' does not contribute very much to an understanding of the process: the religious leaders of Israel, from Moses and Joshua to the temple priests of the post-exilic period, were not concerned with theologically charging the numerical word 'one' – this would become a concern only much later on for Platonizing speculations about the monad.[19] The covenant (*berith*) has the form of a non-mixing contract and a non-translation oath, combined with the highest salvific guarantees. Whoever mixes themselves is eliminated, and whoever translates falls from grace. Thus the ethnogenesis

[19] The meaning of 'one' is unfolded in the course of the Western–Eastern history of ideas: it extends from the one of singularity to the one of the pantheistic cosmos and the theo-mathematically greatest (*maximum et unum*). Remi Brague points out, in *On the God of the Christians (and on One or Two Others)*, trans. Paul Seaton (South Bend, IN: St Augustine's Press, 2013), that the assertion of God's oneness possibly entails a paradoxical implication: while believing oneself to be making God the highest by terming him 'one', this in fact devalues him by subordinating him to the class of unities. Brague distinguishes between three meanings of the 'one' claim: God is one through seamlessness, or being-made-from-one-piece (known in the Qur'an as *assamad*, the impenetrable); he is one through trueness to himself (in the Bible, 'I am that I will be'); he is one through the internal connections of the trinity.

of the Jewish people followed a quite extraordinary autoplastic programme: those belonging to the programme's people were separated from those who did not belong in a constant process of distinction. The new religion of singularization was anything but a naïve folk cult; it was a considered experiment for an ongoing sorting of members and non-members of the covenant. What that meant in real-life terms is revealed by the warning often heard in the Tanakh, specifically in the prophet Isaiah's words, that only a few of those involved at the start would be left. Thus early Jewish history is so far unique in telling not of a people with a religion, as is usually the case, but of a religion with a people. Theologians who are aware of this slightly unnerving finding like to describe it with the word 'chosenness'. By this they mean that it is not enough to have one god or another like all peoples; it is vital to be had by the right god, the unique one.

3

The Sinai Schema:
Integral Swearing-In

In the following, I will look a little more closely
at certain elements of the famous Sinai episode
from the Exodus account in the Pentateuch,
characterizing it as the primal scene of ancient
Jewish anti-miscegenation policy. I will calmly
operate on the assumption that the Sinai account
and the entire construction of the exodus epic,
with its odysseys, rebellions and miracles, is
largely a literary fiction in the mode of *a posteriori*
prophecy, probably written between the eighth
and sixth centuries BC and reworked in the post-
exilic period. I cannot participate in speculations
about the possible inclusion of residues of real
events from earlier epochs in these tales; hence, in
the present essay, the question of geographically

identifying the Sinai location – there seem to be fourteen different hypotheses concerning this – is of no significance. Furthermore, it is no cause for concern that Moses could hardly have brought two stone tablets, inscribed by God's fingers, down from the height of the mountain to the camp of his people. The Münster Old Testament specialist Erich Zenger (1939–2010) wrote the necessary things about this with touching clarity:

> No unique, empirically concrete event of whatever nature becomes visible behind the Sinai accounts in the Book of Exodus: no historical covenant was made at Mount Sinai [. . .] there was no handing over of stone tablets by God to Moses on Mount Sinai. Nor was there [. . .] any fashioning of the Golden Calf by Moses' people or other Sinai Bedouins.[20]

One can conclude that, with no Golden Calf, there was likewise no mass slaughter of dancers around the calf, nor any other religiously

[20] Erich Zenger, *Israel am Sinai: Analysen und Interpretationen zu Exodus 17–34* (Altenberge: CIS, 1982), p. 125.

motivated acts of terror committed by the sup-
porters of Moses against their own people. And
naturally there were no Levites who could have
distinguished themselves in the butchery of the
apostates. The true location of all these events
is purely in the stories themselves. The stories,
for their part, have their vital location in the
'Israelogenic' rites – that is to say, the people-
stabilizing sacrificial acts and text readings that
took place between the eighth and fifth centuries BC in connection with the Jerusalem temple
cult. According to recent archaeological research,
the legendary temple of Solomon was built only
some two hundred years after Solomon's death,
in the mid-eighth century BC, and acted as the
country's cult centre until its destruction by the
troops of Nebuchadnezzar II around 586 BC.
Because no real historical findings can be assigned
to the Sinai stories, the observer must rate their
symbolic significance for the swearing-in of the
people to its religious constitution all the more
highly.

In this context we finally arrive at the question
of how 'monotheism' and violence are connected.
The wording of some passages that will be criti-
cally elucidated will show why there is little to

be gained by identifying the problem of violence primarily as a religio-theoretical construct called 'monotheism', whose evasive meaning I have already pointed out. Instead, the analysis will now foreground the function of the covenantal singularization project with its psychosocial and moral costs.[21] In fact, the account of the breach of covenant by the people of Israel during the absence of Moses on the mountain of God, as described in chapter 32 of the Book of Exodus, provides the unsurpassable paradigm of an act of violence motivated by the singularization contract. The description of it contains one of the most terrible passages of all time in the whole of religious history. When Moses, returning from the mountain, finds the people dancing around the idol amid shouting, he casts the idol down and has it burned, then ground to powder. What remains somewhat mysterious is the religious leader's instruction to scatter the dust of the

[21] In recent times, the costs and price of certain religious constructs have been discussed by such authors as Jan Assmann (*The Price of Monotheism*, trans. Robert Savage [Stanford, CA: Stanford University Press, 2009]) or Elettra Stimilli (*Der Preis des Messianismus: Briefe von Jacob Taubes an Gerschom Scholem und andere Materialien* [Würzburg: Königshausen & Neumann, 2006]).

destroyed calf on the water and force the Israelites to drink it.[22] This is followed by unprecedented butchery:

> So he stood at the entrance to the camp and said, 'Whoever is for the LORD, come to me.' And all the Levites rallied to him.
>
> Then he said to them, 'This is what the LORD, the God of Israel, says: "Each man strap a sword to his side. Go back and forth through the camp from one end to the other, each killing his brother and friend and neighbour."' The Levites did as Moses commanded, and that day about three thousand of the people died.[23]

It has often been noted, and rightly so, that the outbreak of violence described there does not show an 'extraverted', offensive or imperial direction of impact. On the contrary, it is a case of

[22] There have occasionally been attempts to bring light into the darkness of this passage by referring to the ordeal by bitter water for women suspected of infidelity described in Numbers 5: 11–31, which is more likely to increase confusion than to reduce it – unless one connects it to the typical Old Testament language game in which the breach of the covenant is analogous to adultery.

[23] Exodus 32: 26–8 (New International Version).

'inwards-directed violence' – one could almost speak of an auto-genocidal drama. As far as the number of three thousand dead is concerned, it is not easy to decide whether this is a pragmatic or a symbolic number. At any rate, it describes a tremendous amputation performed on the body of the Mosaic people. Indeed, the information that the Levites gathered around Moses permits the assumption that this must have been an act of extermination – always on the site of the imaginary – carried out by the minority faithful to Moses against the majority that followed Aaron. The quoted passage in fact states that the people – one can presumably read this as 'the entire people', except for the officious Levites – took part in the festival of idolatry. One cannot help being amazed that it was the Levites of all people, members of a priestly group, who were at the ready to carry out the divine command. The objection that there cannot yet have been any Levites at that time is of no consequence due to the fictional status of the account. It is then all the more significant that, for lack of real historical content, the tale of the extermination of the temporarily apostate members of the people takes on an outstanding symbolic character – perhaps

even an exemplary dimension.[24] The Levites'
obedience to the Mosaic instruction, however,
meant that they could kill without being murder-
ers. They were breaking the fifth commandment
formally announced a short while earlier (Exodus

---

[24] It is precisely this symbolic and exemplary component of
the document that Rolf Schieder firmly denies in his polemical
remarks about my comments on Exodus 32: 27 in *God's Zeal* –
with inadequate arguments, it seems to me. In his view, Moses'
order was an isolated, politically motivated decision with no
further significance. He seems to consider the fatal reference to
killing brothers and friends a regrettable, but situationally comprehensible command – deliberately passing over the preceding
legitimation 'This is what the LORD, the God of Israel, says'. He
likewise ignores the verse after the passage quoted above, in which
the perpetrators are promised the Lord's blessing. To my mind,
Schieder fails to recognize the archetypal power of the Sinai scene
in the context of the singularization strategy. When he states,
'The readers of this passage never viewed it as anything fundamental' (Rolf Schieder, *Sind Religionen gefährlich?* [Berlin: Berlin
University Press, 2008], p. 78), he is not only claiming more than
he can know, as millions of readers from many generations have
made sense of this 'ghastly text' in unobservable meditations;
most importantly, he fails to see the key role or preformative
effect of the Sinai events for understanding a monotonous series
of episodes recounting divine punitive actions, and their aug-
mentation by zealotic executions, with which the Old Testament
is overflowing. These extend to the auto-genocidal extermination
campaigns of Judas Maccabeus against Jews who were willing to
assimilate in the time of Seleucid Hellenization policies. Even if
one considers all this to be merely overblown priestly literature,
the 'fundamental' or, rather, the programmatic and intentionally
people-forming character of these tales of terror is impossible to
deny.

20), but their deadly actions were subject to a higher law, a form of religious emergency law. It seems that the sword-wielding Levites were acting as successors to the sacred executioners of prehistoric times, whose overwritten traces in several Old Testament passages have recently – however hypothetically – been deciphered.[25]

The decisive insight into the autoplastic, popular pedagogical significance of the Levitic slaughter is offered by the overall structure of the Exodus scenes at Mount Sinai. Their form, which shapes the sequence of events in the separate episodes, corresponds to the traditional narrative triad, which regularly passes through the sequence of initial state, interference incident and restoration. The story's centre of gravity obviously lies in the sealing of the covenant, brokered by Moses, between Yahweh and Israel, whose strength as a means of singularizing their identity amid the competing cults of the polyethnic situation in the Middle East has already been mentioned. In that context, Yahweh still appears with the

[25] See Hyam Maccoby, *The Sacred Executioner: Human Sacrifice and the Legacy of Guilt* (London: Thames & Hudson, 1982).

traits of an invisible tribal chieftain. The relationship between him and his followers is closer to a feudally relevant swearing-in of minions to their feudal lord than a spiritually deepened correspondence between God and the people, let alone God and the individual soul.

After the failure of Israel's attempts, during the royal period inaugurated by David (1012–597 BC), to intervene in the concert of regional empire-formations between Mesopotamia with its own state creations, the religious leaders of the people must have decided to take greater recourse to covenant-theological thought figures. These had, admittedly, also been kept alive in early prophetic literature through occasional interventions.

The pathos of self-isolation inevitably experienced immense growth as a result of the disaster-conditioned boom in covenant theology after the catastrophe of 597 BC – as these stories from Exodus show. This is emphatically reflected by the structure of the Sinai account, in which we encounter not only the narrative triad of the sealing of the covenant (Exodus 19: 24), the breach of covenant (Exodus 32) and then the restoration of the covenant (Exodus 34), which seems obligatory for a resolution of a good story in keeping with the laws of narration. In addition, the exorbitant violence of the middle part, which depicts the irruption of interference, reveals how willing the narrators of the Sinai drama were to immerse themselves in the problem – which had always been virulent, but now constituted a more gaping abyss than ever – of the breach of covenant. The talked-up breach of covenant at Mount Sinai, then, is not simply a cult-historical episode that gives pious minds food for thought; it is of a prototypical character. The thought of it – and the constant danger of its repetition – develops into an obsession; more still, it grows into a thought form that virtually promises its users the key to the dark vicissitudes of Israel's history.

I therefore refer to the obsessively recurring motif of the breach of covenant as the 'Sinai schema'. It makes the price of Israel's singularization amid the intense cultic and military competition between peoples palpable. In the fictional primal scene at the foot of the mountain of God, the motivic connection between the breach of the covenant and the summary trial was displayed with archetypal power and made available for transference to any remote context. It supplies the prototype of a 'connection between deeds and consequences', to recall the technical term popular among Old Testament experts.[26] With the help of the Sinai schema – the breach of covenant results in punishment by extermination, then the journey continues with the 'rest' – it becomes virtually possible to read the history of Israel both forwards and backwards, especially where, as during Babylonian exile, it was experienced or interpreted as a history of misfortune. While the extermination at Mount Sinai followed the manifest breach of covenant at a brief interval and following a linear logic, later, initially inexplicable ordeals suffered by the people can be attributed only indirectly to what remained a latent breach of covenant. This latter was usually recognized only by the prophets and priests, who traced a path backwards from the manifest punitive suffering to the latent offence. The concept of sin itself, without which the course of the Jewish, Christian and Islamic history of ideas, feelings and cults is unimaginable, is coloured from the start by the ever-present danger of a breach of

[26] See Klaus Koch. 'Is There a Doctrine of Retribution in the Old Testament?', in J. L. Crenshaw (ed.), *Theodicy in the Old Testament* (Philadelphia: Fortress, 1983), pp. 57–87.

covenant. Essentially, every sin is a regression to life before the Sinaite conversion. Each individual sin refreshes the primary sin of betraying the covenantal duty, indeed almost of betraying God, with varying explicitness.

Readers of the Bible will encounter an early and typical application of the Sinai schema in chapter 25 of the Book of Numbers (*Bamidbar*). It recounts how the people of Israel, while encamped at Shittim (probably in eastern Jordan), began to 'indulge in sexual immorality with Moabite women' and participated in sacrifices to the Moabite 'gods'. The consequences were predictable:

> The LORD said to Moses, 'Take all the leaders of these people, kill them and expose them in broad daylight before the LORD, so that the LORD's fierce anger may turn away from Israel.'
>
> So Moses said to Israel's judges, 'Each of you must put to death those of your men who have joined in worshipping the Baal of Peor.'[27]

---

[27] Numbers 25: 4–5; concerning the motif of hanging corpses on poles, see Gunnar Heinsohn, *Die Erschaffung der Götter: Das Opfer als Ursprung der Religion* (Reinbek: Rowohlt, 1997).

Here too, as at Sinai, the general ban on killing is replaced by a higher duty to kill – an exemption that in these cases does not follow from any warrior ethics but, rather, imposes itself as an inevitable consequence of the breach of covenant. Furthermore, the same passage reports that a plague broke out among the Israelites, claiming 24,000 lives. The pestilence, whose punitive character becomes evident in retrospect, ended only when Phinehas, a grandson of the priest Aaron, discovered the source of evil when he took his spear and ran through an Israelite who had slept with a Midianite woman.

> The LORD said to Moses, 'Phinehas [. . .] has turned my anger away from the Israelites [. . .]. Therefore tell him I am making my covenant of peace with him. He and his descendants will have a covenant of a lasting priesthood, because he was zealous for the honour of his God and made atonement for the Israelites.'[28]

In the light of all this, it goes without saying that the priests of Israel considered the decades

[28] Numbers 25: 10–13.

of Babylonian exile a punishment for a latent chronic breach of covenant. Incidentally, recent research contradicts the priestly myth of the Jewish people sighing under the yoke of captivity. Many members of Israel's upper class felt quite at ease in their colourful place of exile, which was almost like a Mesopotamian New York; they enjoyed freedoms of all kinds, and it is no coincidence that they remained there even after the fall of Babylon. Only after the Arab–Israeli war of 1948 were its modern descendants driven out of the area, which would soon be named Iraq.

It is impossible to imagine the overall finding of the Sinai schema without the cultically explicated duty to be cruel, which was meant to be demonstrated by the execution of severe commands from God or human leaders. Thus Moses orders the warriors to exterminate the Midianites completely when they exact vengeance for the seduction. He is angered by the news that the Israelite army killed only all the men, taking the women and children prisoner. In his zeal, fuelled by awareness of the covenant, Moses insists on killing all boys and grown women too, sparing only the virgin girls: 'save for yourselves every girl who has never slept with a man' (Numbers

31: 18). In the subsequent Israelite conquest, the Jewish armies are given the task of preventatively exterminating the local populations of Amorites, Canaanites, Perizzites, Hivites and Jebusites so that they cannot even tempt the still impressionable covenant people 'to follow all the detestable things they do in worshipping their gods'.[29] The danger of the breach of covenant accompanies the further history of the mandatorily zealous programme people with varying degrees of explicitness. The Deuteronomist maxim 'show them no mercy' is often invoked when dealing with 'unbelievers' and tempters.[30] Naturally the gruesome acts of Judas Maccabeus, son of the priest Mattathias, in his extermination programmes against fellow Jews who were willing to assimilate during the struggle for Jewish cult freedom in the second century BC, consistently follow the principles of the zealous culture founded at Mount Sinai. The Books of the Maccabees tell proudly of Judas's acts of violence against members of his own people.

In summary, one can say that the admonition

[29] Deuteronomy 20: 18.
[30] Deuteronomy 7: 2.

to preserve the covenant unconditionally always entails the strictest cultic duty. Whoever fails to celebrate Passover (unless on a journey and away from the cult community) 'must be cut off from his people because he did not present the LORD's offering at the appointed time.'[31] 'Whoever sacrifices to any god other than the LORD must be destroyed.'[32] 'Anyone who desecrates [the Sabbath] must be put to death.'[33] These expressions of severity towards unbelievers and foreigners did not survive in the text as relics of titanic crudity; one must view them as deliberate warning signs. They dramatize the connection between simple sin and breach of covenant: the danger of apostasy is always already at hand. The frequently pondered and redacted brutalisms of the Holy Scripture, which probably reached its final state around 400 BC, can only be understood through their religious grammar. For this one must become aware of the psychopolitical peculiarity that what they express is by no means a cheerful primary aggressiveness, an ingenuous

[31] Numbers 9: 13.
[32] Exodus 22: 20.
[33] Exodus 31: 14.

expansionism or a naïve ethnocentrism. They are derivatives of the precarious prerogative of severity towards oneself that, read positively, we call chosenness.

4

Phobocracy:
On the Proliferation of the
Principle of Total Membership

In the following, I would like to return to the frequently voiced assumption that the words of violence quoted above were for the most part of a literary, performative and evocative nature. I maintain that they amounted only to vehement verbalisms that were not followed by any real actions in most cases. In practical religious and ethno-pedagogical terms, they belonged to the speech acts of swearing-in with which the people of Israel reflected on the foundations of their 'special existence'.[34] It is not without reason that Jan Assmann, in his Vienna lecture *Monotheism and*

[34] Zenger, *Israel am Sinai*, p. 156.

the Language of Force,[35] referred to the linguistic conditions of the new *modus vivendi* that rested on the divine covenant. Its revolutionary novelty could only be articulated in a language of collective conversion. Under the singularizing effect of the Sinai schema, an entire people attempted for the first time to adopt the mode of being of a zealous collective, or of salvation-concerned implementers of the law. The language forms of this mode of existence encompass, on the one hand, the declaration of salvation and the words of blessing, self-congratulation and thanks – it is to these that religious world literature owes some of the highest documents of theopoetic speech. On the other hand, the gestures of announcing disaster, cursing oneself and others, the warning speech and the expression of repentance ('a broken and contrite heart, O God, you will not despise')[36] accumulate to form a stream of constant self-admonition, even self-frightening. Assmann rightly states that 'exclusive monotheism' – I would rather say the singularizing

[35] Jan Assmann, *Monotheismus und die Sprache der Gewalt* (Vienna: Picus, 2006).
[36] Psalm 51: 17.

43

strategy in the competition between cults and peoples – intrinsically requires a 'semantics of rupture, of demarcation, of conversion'.[37]

What rupture, demarcation and conversion have in common is that they constitute aspects of a new culture of total membership.[38] Certainly early tribes and peoples, on the whole, naturally possess the character of total institutions for their members, and a meaningful life can scarcely be imagined outside of them – which is why banishment often amounted to a psychosocial death penalty. But the old ethnic formations, as recent ethnology stresses, were usually far more open to interactions with other peoples, to absorptions, assimilations and mixtures, than the romantic assertion of substantial ethnicities wishes to believe. The Sinai schema – for the first time, as far as one can see – elevates a people to a programmatic total institution that imposes on its members, along with the strictest ban on miscegenation, the duty to integral membership in a sublime cultic-ethical project.

[37] Assmann, *Monotheismus und die Sprache der Gewalt*, p. 51.
[38] I have chosen the word 'membership' over alternatives such as 'belonging' in order to emphasize sharing and participation rather than possessive aspects.

It is chiefly to this ethnogenetic stroke of genius, this singular transformation of a chance ethnicity from previously inconspicuous 'idolatrous' tribe into a zealous programme people under the one God, that the impressive phenomenon of 'Judaism's survival over time'[39] must be attributed. What has been known since early times as the 'fence around the Torah', and more recently as the fence of norms around the Jewish people, is nothing other than the result of applying the Sinai schema to the ethnic substrate of the Exodus people, who were later – at the assembly of Shechem[40] – joined by a number of non-Exodus tribes.[41] It was these historically impressive effects of Judaism's self-enclosure through scriptural piety and obedience to laws that inspired Heinrich

[39] See Peter Daniel, *Zaun: Normen als Zaum um das jüdische Volk: Zum Phänomen des Judentums* (Vienna: Edition Splitter, 1995).

[40] Joshua 24.

[41] One reason for the significance of the assembly of Shechem is that it presents the first cases of covenant renewal through a covenant extension to former non-members, while the covenant renewal at Mount Sinai applied exclusively to the survivors of the Golden Calf apostasy. With this, the mythical quality of the phrase 'led out of Egypt' becomes fully manifest: after Shechem, it refers mostly to groups whose descendants cannot have taken part in the exodus, even at a fictional level.

Heine to the equally elegant and profound remark
that, for the Jews of the diaspora period, the Bible
was a 'portable homeland'.

The Sinaite singularization strategy consisted
primarily of a considerable number of self-
inclusion measures whose aim was to establish
the most insurmountable difference between
inside and outside – a difference whose pure
realization is doubly endangered: from within,
through the ever-present risk of apostasy, starting with an indifference to tradition, and from
without, through repressions and offers of assimilation from foreign powers. A substantial part of
the religious people's life takes the form of quar-
rels at the fence.

Where the fence is erected around the people
in 'special existence', not only through repeated
promises but also by the means of chronic self-
admonition, the ordinary political phobocracy
that was essential to the formation of larger, hier-
archically structured systems of domination from
ancient times onwards changes into a new form
of fear control with primarily inward effects.
It gives the people affected a manner of auto-
phobocratic constitution. In this constitution,
the general religious aversion to numinous things

and the vengeance of the gods takes a special form: the fear of a covenant breach and its consequences. Because virtually every offence can be viewed against the background of the breach of covenant in this regime because it violates holy norms, punishments took on a phobocratic character even in low-ranking matters. The Book of Deuteronomy (*Devarim*) in the Pentateuch discusses the case of a disobedient and drunken son who is to be dealt with in the following way: his parents must apprehend him and bring him to the court gate. 'Then all the men of his town shall stone him to death. You must purge the evil from among you. All Israel will hear of it and be afraid.'[42] In the climate of generalized phobocracy, the effects of the Sinai schema advance to the level of everyday conflict. The body of biblical sayings reflects this in the maxim 'The fear of the LORD is the beginning of wisdom.'[43]

In the zone affected by the strictly applied Sinai schema, the psyche of the believers comes under

[42] Deuteronomy 21: 21.

[43] Psalm III: 10. For a Darwin-inspired and mnemopolitical interpretation of the connections between religion, fear and terror, see Heiner Mühlmann, *Jesus überlistet Darwin* (Vienna and New York: Springer, 2007).

47

the influence of a confusing twofold demand best described as a phobocratic paradox. This makes no small contribution to the development of that religiously tense inwardness that springs from constantly toiling away at unsolvable riddles.[44] Under the impression of the Sinaite primal scene, the believers find themselves confronted with the self-contradictory command to have unconditional faith in God's mercy because otherwise God will mercilessly exterminate them. This can only result in a habitus in which trust is reshaped by the fear of fear. After that, the bright side of faith can only be attained by suppressing all thoughts of the sinister side. This pattern is still evident in Saint Paul's concept of faith.

It would be a grave mistake to assume that the effects of the Sinai schema were restricted to the religious constitution of Israel in pre-modern times. If there are genuinely good reasons to speak of a group of eminent monotheistic religions and their problematic relationship with the question of violence, it is because the basic

---

[44] Concerning this, see the section 'Paradoxes and Passions: The Genesis of the Inner World through Chronic Overstraining' in *You Must Change Your Life*, pp. 273–5.

structures of the Sinaite constitution were passed on to Judaism's religious successors, namely Christianity and Islam – not in every respect, but in a number of important elements. The history of both Christianity and Islam can be understood, to a certain degree, as the migration of the Sinai schema through expansive non-Jewish collective projects. Only in these did the familiar massive discharges of violence take place, directed both inwards and outwards, that cast their shadow on religious history. It would therefore seem productive to define the trio of classical monotheisms in terms of the shared model of the Sinai schema, regardless of the fact that many theologians prefer the post-anti-Semitic phantom concept of the 'Abrahamic religions', to which they owe many an enjoyable hour at the ecumenical fireplace. In fact, going back to Abraham as the supposed source of inter-monotheistic commonality misses the decisive ethnogenetic point: the aura of the covenant between Yahweh and Abraham, sealed when the latter was ninety-nine, is still that of the patriarchal fairy tale; despite the dark story of Isaac, it still has the charm of the pre-Sinaite Israel that Thomas Mann memorialized in his tetralogy *Joseph and His Brothers*. Abraham's covenant is formulated as a promise of faith to a pious individual, despite the talk of being blessed with countless descendants. It does not yet have the element of Sinaite escalation that takes effect with the collective revelation at the mountain of God, and with the enlistment of an entire people to make a contract of obedience with God.

What Christianity and Islam have in common with Judaism is not their mythical origin in a shared forefather but, rather, the new ethnogenetic form that separates them from the other ethnic groups as programme peoples with prophetic scripts. The Sinaite programme people of Israel found their true kin and typological successors in the pneumatic programme people known in Christian parlance as the *ekklesia* and in the Quranic programme people that constitute themselves as *umma wahidāh*, the one community of Muslims. The precondition for both new peoples was an escape from the ethnic retreat of Judaism.

The three theogenic collectives share something first developed clearly in the escalation of Sinai, namely an access to the life of their adherents in the mode of total membership – whether one calls it *qana* in Hebrew, *zélos* in Greek or *jihad* in Arabic. This is evident not least in their shared profound nervousness about the danger of apostasy. It would be rash to view the problem of apostasy in the resolute programme peoples in terms of individuals leaving the church in a modernized society. In fact, the two religions that succeeded Judaism likewise – following the Sinai schema – consider departure from a salvific community a breach of covenant, even if the covenant partners are no longer Yahweh and Israel but the Three-in-One and his church people or Allah and his Muslim community. It is therefore hardly surprising that, in the times of their social authority, the total programme collectives could *de jure* send death sentences after their 'defectors' or those tired of religion, or at least an eschatological curse and heartfelt ill-will. Even today, Islam is virtually obsessed with the problem of apostasy (*ridda*), as demonstrated by – among other things – a fatal judgement of the fatwa committee at al-Azhar University in Cairo (the most revered institution in Sunni Islam) from 1978, which states that, under certain circumstances, apostates must still be killed as traitors to Allah. In addition, contemporary Islam is afflicted more than ever by suspicions of real or alleged blasphemies. As members of a zealous collective whose members sense their own cultural weaknesses with increasing clarity, some modern-day Muslim zealots miss no opportunity to feel offended by unbelievers. They respond to these attacks, many of them imagined or eagerly awaited, with a zealotic reinforcement of boundaries.

Anyone interested in methods of producing total membership in the early twenty-first century need only acquaint themselves with the activities of Taliban schools in Afghanistan and Wahhabi centres of education in Saudi Arabia, whose graduates become most visible in the countries of Africa and Asia. And one cannot keep silent about the fact that similar things go on in some European backyard mosques. Those interested should, however, also inform themselves about the universities of Protestant sects in the USA, seminaries of the Pius Brotherhood in Switzerland, and the Opus Angelorum and Marian fervour societies in Bavaria, as well as the dealings of countless totalitarian mini-religions all over the world; for all their differences, the one thing they all share is that, in an apparently old-fashioned manner, they reach for the 'entire existence' of their members.

5

Metamorphoses of Membership

It is in the nature of modern societies that, in the course of their functional differentiation, they relieve religious semantics (and religious ritualistics) from the task of collective synthesis. Societies can be considered modern as soon as they create cohesion through secular media and functionally separated, interlocking subsystems without having to develop a true self or cult centre at a particular point – not even in the parliaments or sociology departments. In this way, they free up religion as a whole to concentrate on its 'main business': the interpretation of being-in-the-world as such – which it pursues in irresolvable rivalry with art and philosophy – coming to terms with fate and attending to the last things. Among believers who think back nostalgically to pre-modern conditions, this liberation is experienced as a loss of meaning. The great majority of those affected by religion would have experienced the end of intrusive collectivizations in the name of imposed cult and church membership as a form of relief. This shows that, for structural reasons, the real or systemic 'reformation' of religious life could not yet take place in the century of Luther and Calvin, as the period was capable of producing only alternative forms of religious totalism – as the integrist escalations of Lutheranism and Calvinism demonstrate. It took place in any substantial sense only between the eighteenth and twentieth centuries, through the differentiation of religion into a 'subsystem' with functions based on its own laws.

This is the reformation that even the Roman Catholic Church, despite intense anti-liberal resistance, was unable to reject. Even after the historic compromise with 'liberalism' at the Second Vatican Council, however, it still displayed unmistakable counter-reformatory tendencies in the form of neo-Sinaite intensifications: it is no coincidence that Benedict XVI recently reminded the Church of its true identity as a pneumatic people of witnesses and urged them to turn away from the world more thoroughly.[45] As it has long been unable to play the part of a collective-forming state church, the only remaining possibility on the path of turning away from the world is self-assurance in a parallel society animated by pneuma and dogma – which does not rule out a later opening to the world.

From a systems-evolutionary perspective, it is certainly understandable that, in the transition from traditional societies with a unified religioid semantics to modern societies with discrete 'basic values'[46] – especially in the first half of the twentieth century – the problem of so-called substitute religions had to arise. The things termed nationalism, totalitarianism, fascism, communism, fundamentalism or integrism were and are, in essence, nothing other than varyingly desperate attempts to re-enact earlier forms of collective synthesis offered by omnicompetent religion

[45] This was said in his speech at the Freiburg Konzerthaus on 25 September 2011.

[46] See Niklas Luhmann, 'Grundwerte als Zivilreligion: Zur wissenschaftlichen Karriere eines Themas', in *Soziologische Aufklärung*, vol. 3: *Soziales System, Gesellschaft, Organisation* (Opladen: Westdeutscher Verlag, 1981), pp. 293–308.

with new, semi-arbitrary themes such as national culture, socialization of the means of production, Fuehrer cult, racial difference or literalism. In the systemic 'reformation', bourgeois art religion – despite some questionable exaggerations – took over a generally productive role, as it offered the possibility of using aesthetic cult objects for rehearsing the transition from a traditional cult practice based on forced membership to spontaneous, dogma-less forms of worship.

The structural change of the religious in modernity could not fail to influence the forms of total membership that had developed after the ethnogenetic stroke of genius at Mount Sinai. Thus it affects the former, continuing Israelization of Israel under ritual law as much as its parallels in the programme peoples of the Christian churches and Islam, which, each in their own way, had devoted themselves to the constant Christianization of Christians and the Islamization of Muslims. Clearly an emancipation took place in Western Judaism, starting in the eighteenth century, that leads beyond the communal constraints of the past and the chronic suspicion of the breach of covenant. On the Jewish path to ethical liberalism, a serious approach to democracy can be considered a continuation of the covenant by other means.[47]

In the course of modernization, such concepts as membership or belonging are subjected to profound revision. There are essentially two changes in the social system that deprive the phenomenon of total membership in religious groups of its foundation: firstly, the aforementioned release of traditional religion from the business of collective synthesis (which also involves dealing with some forms of the once inescapable 'political theology')[48] and, secondly, the progressive elevation of individuals to bearers of inalienable

[47] When Avishai Margalit writes, 'Most modern Jews lost their faith without even for a moment losing their sense of being Jews' (*Apostasie*, ed. Volker Drehsen [Tübingen: Mohr Siebeck, 2012], p. 58), he is summarizing the result of a collective loss of religion that need no longer be classified as apostasy or breach of covenant, provided those concerned have remained within a continuum of ethnic loyalties and basic ethical orientations.

[48] When in 1935 Erik Peterson drew on the Church's concept of essence to prove the impossibility of political theology, he failed to notice the latter's tendency to be made superfluous by the evolutionary reconstruction of the social structure. Like all his contemporaries, he was prevented from seeing the larger processual context by the predominance of the typical political substitute religions of the time, and also by the disastrous compromises of the actually existing churches with those after 1933. See Erik Peterson, 'Monotheism as a Political Problem', in *Theological Tractates* (Stanford, CA: Stanford University Press, 2011).

basic rights. Among these, the rights to free movement and choice of religion stand out.[49] Even if
it is an exaggeration to speak of a sacralization
of the person in modernity, the sovereignization
of the person is an undeniable fact.[50] By provid-
ing a counterweight rooted in basic law to the
potentially demonically heightenable idea of the
people's sovereignty, it *eo ipso* does away with
the collective's access to individuals, emancipat-
ing them from the imposition of total belonging
to a people. Overall, the concept of the people
becomes increasingly problematic – indeed, the
ethnicities themselves increasingly seem anach-
ronistic, at times no more than venerable bulky
items in the material and informatics streams of
global society. Observations with this tendency
were anticipated by Karl Marx in his still offensive remarks on the Jewish question, in which
he put the case for a dissolution of the separate
people in a humanity emancipated by the release
of productive powers.

[49] See the Universal Declaration of Human Rights (1948),
sections 13 and 18.
[50] See Hans Joas, *The Sacredness of the Person: A New
Genealogy of Human Rights*, trans. Alex Skinner (Washington,
DC: Georgetown University Press, 2013).

These developments virtually suspended the imposition of total membership emanating from the collective that resembled a religious people. In modern society, membership is understood as fundamentally optional, on the one hand, and as fundamentally plural, on the other. At the level of modern assurances of basic rights, the right to leave a nation is as undisputed as the duty of a cult membership: emigration is not treason, and leaving the Church is not punishable apostasy, even if the latter results in excommunication and a loss of the right to pay church taxes. Only in the case of war (more precisely, a people's war) do modern nation states, in so far as they still impose universal military service, regress to a condition of forced collectivity with obligatory sacrifices.

Against the background of the structural change of membership, the continued survival of older and renovated forms of total membership becomes a special problem of modernity. The discourses on so-called religious fundamentalisms, most of them conceptually helpless, have referred to this for some time. Similarly, the even more helpless question 'Are religions dangerous?', which some theologians pose to reassure themselves of their interesting profession, reacts to the no longer repressible fact that, alongside the complicated, yet often successful liberal life forms of partial and multiple membership in ethnic, religious, professional and other collectives, there are still – or once again – tendencies towards monolithic or mono-membership life forms. In those, for example, it becomes questionable whether one can be both a Muslim *and* a citizen of a Western nation state without hypocrisy.

I read the question of the old or new dangerousness of religion as expressing a typically modern problem that can be described as the tolerance paradox: whereas a strict imperative of intolerance was in force during the predominance of the Sinai schema – as a necessary implication of the ban on miscegenation, assimilation and shared sacrifices – a central feature of the liberal order of things is the imperative of tolerance, with or without recourse to the Parable of the Ring.[51] This includes tolerance towards the intolerant. It testifies to the admirable strength of the religio-liberal way of life that it is willing to put up with almost all surviving or newly grown forms of zealotry; only its terroristic escalations are exempted from indulgence. Ethical

---

[51] See *God's Zeal*, ch. 7, 'The Parables of the Ring', pp. 122–50.

liberalism declares the preference of individuals for ways of living under a high level of normative self-constraint to be a private matter of these constraint-lovers and remains largely neutral in its approach to their declarations. It is one of the ironies of religions in modernity that they even make the absolute an option. Even those struggling to achieve orthodoxy do not escape the heretical imperative, for true belief too depends on a choice (*hairesis*) in its favour.

Nowhere can the robustness of the liberal arrangement be better observed than in the respectful way in which the state of Israel, founded in 1948 and formally neutral in religious terms, treats its zealous citizens by paying state pensions to the ultraorthodox, even though some of them dispute the legitimacy of this very state, partly with convincing religion-immanent arguments. It is as if, despite its predominantly secular orientation, it had some understanding for the fact that the daily observance of 365 prohibitions and 248 duties of ancient Jewish piety is a full-time job that is compatible with neither employment nor military service or political office. Only a modernity that still supports those who reject it lives up to its own standard.

In the light of all this, it is clear that the main work in the dissolution of traditions of total membership was done by the systemic reconstruction of modernizing society when the latter shifted from politically motivated confessional coercion to free choice of cult. At the socio-political level, this corresponded to the structural change of the 'people' into the 'population' and the descent of ethnic characteristics into folklore. The relevant classifications for human associations 'after peoples' are masses, mob, multitude and the silent majority.[52] In relation to these factors, the question of God and gods is silenced.

The approach to the remnants of intolerance that survived the turn towards the subsystemization of religion remains an open task. The phrase 'civilization of religions through education' describes it fairly accurately.[53] Whether

[52] See in this context Christian Borch, *The Politics of Crowds: An Alternative History of Sociology* (Cambridge: Cambridge University Press, 2012), ch. 8, 'Postmodern Conditions: The Rise of the Post-Political Masses', pp. 269f. Following on from Michel Maffesoli's reflections on the 'new tribes', the author shows how far the current pluralism of idols is from all conventional theological concepts. Even the term 'polytheism' can only be applied metaphorically to the swarming of hedonistic themed clubs and fan bases.

[53] Rolf Schieder, *Sind Religionen gefährlich?*, pp. 274f. I gave

the newly popular football matches between imams and vicars can contribute to the education programmes that are desirable to that end, however, is uncertain. The recently increased polemics of Christian theologians against supposed postmodern polytheism are certainly not educationally effective. Mocking the memory of 'cosmotheism' in non-monotheistic religions is anti-educational. Religious thinkers suggested more reliable methods of civilization between the sixteenth and twentieth centuries, some of which are more informative than ever.

It seems to me that five of these approaches currently merit particular emphasis. The first is the domestication of zealotry in the 'Erasmus mode', which is still connected today to the memory of a civilizing synthesis of humanistic and Christian motifs. It is no coincidence that programmes for an Erasmian Europe are a focus of current educational policy. This is followed

some intimations in chapter 6 ('The Pharmaka') of my essay on the conflict between the three monotheisms as to how the zeal for God can be reduced with the aid of polyvalent logic, thinking in stages, hermeneutics and humour. I could have added the ordinarization of the cult, which *per se* ensures conviviality and relaxation.

by the 'Spinoza mode', in which the sublation
of jealously guarded vested rights into univer-
sally accessible philosophical insights is brought
forward aggressively for the first time – not
without mocking the parish-pump politics of
the historical religions. The third approach is
the great religio-psychologically civilizing inter-
vention in the 'James mode', which presented
itself in the Gifford Lectures given from 1901 to
1902 on *The Varieties of Religious Experience*.[54] In
his open empiricism, the psychologist William
James offered an example of how an undogmatic
interest in religion, whether as a 'will to believe'
or as a humanizing scepticism, outstrips the zeal
of conventional religious forced collectives. Next,
contributions to religious theory in the 'Scholem
mode' might also prove to have a great civilizing
effect; Scholem discovered heresy, especially in
Judaism, as the innermost driving force of religious evolution and understood it as a constant,
inevitable and creative struggle between heretical and orthodox forces.[55] This angle of enquiry

[54] William James, *The Varieties of Religious Experience*
(Cambridge, MA: Harvard University Press, 1985).
[55] Scholem's research focused especially on the heretical
messianism of the Kabbalah; see Christoph Schmidt, *Der häre-*

should prove equally rewarding for the study of non-Jewish religious systems. At the dawn of the twenty-first century, finally, the civilizing religious discourse experienced a further revival in the 'Assmann mode'. This showed how, starting from Egyptian beginnings, a common thread of ideas about the possibility and reality of dual religion runs through European tradition – the exoteric and esoteric, the popular and the philosophical, the local and the universal, the outer and the inner, the political and the natural.[56]

With these mentors at our side, we can traverse the craggy landscape of new religious polemics a little more sure-footedly. We can learn from them that religion and religions – which should finally be better understood as mental and ritual practising systems – have always been, and still are, important manifestations of poetic human habitation on the earth, especially once mostly

tische Imperativ: Überlegungen zur theologischen Dialektik der Kulturwissenschaften in Deutschland (Tübingen: Mohr Siebeck, 2000). Schmidt offers, among other things, an informative comparison between the theological ideas of Carl Schmitt and Gershom Scholem.

[56] See Jan Assmann, Religio Duplex: How the Enlightenment Reinvented Egyptian Religion, trans. Robert Savage (Cambridge: Polity, 2014).

relieved of their ethnogenic functions (to the advantage of all, in my opinion). I have suggested elsewhere that the conventional discipline of theology should be separated, with one half assigned to the theatre studies or poetics and the other to general training studies – the latter are termed 'general' because, in them, all cultures and cultivations are allocated to the field of active and passive phenomena of repetition and practice. This approach would do far greater justice to the historical power and still tangible virulence of the human spirit's theopoetic achievements than is currently possible in the demarcations of instituted faculties.

One of the most remarkable effects of globally active theopoetics is not least the existence of historical peoples – and their survival into the present, in however broken a form. In a conversation with Count Reventlow, Frederick the Great allegedly asked, 'Can you name a single unrefuted proof of God's existence?' Reventlow is said to have answered, 'Yes, Your Majesty, the Jews!' Perhaps a proof of God's existence through a people would be too much to ask, but the proof of a people's existence through the adherence to a god can be considered given. Whether proofs of

people's existence will one day be possible without violence, and whether they might indeed
become superfluous at some point, will transpire
only in a distant future.

Index